I0804727

SONG OF SONGS

REFORMED EXPOSITORY BIBLE STUDIES

A Companion Series to the Reformed Expository Commentaries

Series Editors

Daniel M. Doriani
Iain M. Duguid
Richard D. Phillips
Philip Graham Ryken

1 Samuel: A King after God's Own Heart
Esther & Ruth: The Lord Delivers and Redeems
Song of Songs: Friendship on Fire
Daniel: Faith Enduring through Adversity
Matthew: Making Disciples for the Nations (two volumes)
Luke: Knowing for Sure (two volumes)
Galatians: The Gospel of Free Grace
Ephesians: The Glory of Christ in the Life of the Church
Philippians: To Live Is Christ
Hebrews: Standing Firm in Christ
James: Portrait of a Living Faith

Forthcoming

John: The Word Incarnate (two volumes)

SONG OF SONGS

FRIENDSHIP ON FIRE

A 13-LESSON STUDY

REFORMED EXPOSITORY
BIBLE STUDY

JON NIELSON
and **IAIN M. DUGUID**

P&R
PUBLISHING
P.O. BOX 817 • PHILLIPSBURG • NEW JERSEY 08865-0817

© 2022 by P&R Publishing

All rights reserved. No part of this book may be reproduced, stored in a retrieval system, or transmitted in any form or by any means—electronic, mechanical, photocopy, recording, or otherwise—except for brief quotations for the purpose of review or comment, without the prior permission of the publisher, P&R Publishing Company, P.O. Box 817, Phillipsburg, New Jersey 08865–0817.

Unless otherwise indicated, Scripture quotations are from the *ESV® Bible* (*The Holy Bible, English Standard Version®*), Copyright © 2001 by Crossway, a publishing ministry of Good News Publishers. Used by permission. All rights reserved.

Scripture quotations marked (TOTC), as well as those that are taken from the Song of Songs within the boxed quotations, are from Iain M. Duguid, *The Song of Songs: An Introduction and Commentary*, TOTC 19 (Downers Grove, IL: InterVarsity Press, 2015).

All boxed quotations are taken from Iain M. Duguid's *Song of Songs* in the Reformed Expository Commentary series. Page numbers in quotations refer to that source.

ISBN: 978-1-62995-933-7 (pbk)
ISBN: 978-1-62995-934-4 (ePub)

Printed in the United States of America

CONTENTS

SERIES INTRODUCTION

Studying the Bible will change your life. This is the consistent witness of Scripture and the experience of people all over the world, in every period of church history.

King David said, "The law of the Lord is perfect, reviving the soul; the testimony of the Lord is sure, making wise the simple; the precepts of the Lord are right, rejoicing the heart; the commandment of the Lord is pure, enlightening the eyes" (Ps. 19:7–8). So anyone who wants to be wiser and happier, and who wants to feel more alive, with a clearer perception of spiritual reality, should study the Scriptures.

Whether we study the Bible alone or with other Christians, it will change us from the inside out. The Reformed Expository Bible Studies provide tools for biblical transformation. Written as a companion to the Reformed Expository Commentary, this series of short books for personal or group study is designed to help people study the Bible for themselves, understand its message, and then apply its truths to daily life.

Each Bible study is introduced by a pastor-scholar who has written a full-length expository commentary on the same book of the Bible. The individual chapters start with the summary of a Bible passage, explaining **The Big Picture** of this portion of God's Word. Then the questions in **Getting Started** introduce one or two of the passage's main themes in ways that connect to life experience. These questions may be especially helpful for group leaders in generating lively conversation.

Understanding the Bible's message starts with seeing what is actually there, which is where **Observing the Text** comes in. Then the Bible study provides a longer and more in-depth set of questions entitled **Understanding the Text**. These questions carefully guide students through the entire passage, verse by verse or section by section.

It is important not to read a Bible passage in isolation, but to see it in the wider context of Scripture. So each Bible study includes two **Bible Connections** questions that invite readers to investigate passages from other places in Scripture—passages that add important background, offer valuable contrasts or comparisons, and especially connect the main passage to the person and work of Jesus Christ.

The next section is one of the most distinctive features of the Reformed Expository Bible Studies. The authors believe that the Bible teaches important doctrines of the Christian faith, and that reading biblical literature is enhanced when we know something about its underlying theology. The questions in **Theology Connections** identify some of these doctrines by bringing the Bible passage into conversation with creeds and confessions from the Reformed tradition, as well as with learned theologians of the church.

Our aim in all of this is to help ordinary Christians apply biblical truth to daily life. **Applying the Text** uses open-ended questions to get people thinking about sins that need to be confessed, attitudes that need to change, and areas of new obedience that need to come alive by the power and influence of the Holy Spirit. Finally, each study ends with a **Prayer Prompt** that invites Bible students to respond to what they are learning with petitions for God's help and words of praise and gratitude.

You will notice boxed quotations throughout the Bible study. These quotations come from one of the volumes in the Reformed Expository Commentary. Although the Bible study can stand alone and includes everything you need for a life-changing encounter with a book of the Bible, it is also intended to serve as a companion to a full commentary on the same biblical book. Reading the full commentary is especially useful for teachers who want to help their students answer the questions in the Bible study at a deeper level, as well as for students who wish to further enrich their own biblical understanding.

The people who worked together to produce this series of Bible studies have prayed that they will engage you more intimately with Scripture, producing the kind of spiritual transformation that only the Bible can bring.

Philip Graham Ryken
Coeditor of the Reformed Expository Commentary series

INTRODUCING THE SONG OF SONGS

Throughout its history, the Song of Songs has been regarded as a challenging book to understand, and it has always had two broad schools of interpretation: one that reads it primarily as a description of the relationship between God and his people, and one that reads it primarily as a text that honors the value and significance of human love and sexuality. Each interpretive school has had representatives who follow a serious grammatical-historical approach, alongside others who discover by free association all kinds of potential applications in its beautiful imagery. The approach followed in this study will be to see the Song as belonging to the genre of wisdom literature—a genre that often speaks about God's design for human relationships, which are a key part of wise living in this world. It is no surprise, then, that an entire book of the Bible is devoted to the most important of those relationships: marriage.

The **main purpose** of the book is to affirm the importance and value of love and sex within the limits of an exclusive marital relationship between one man and one woman. The book contrasts this with other, competing views of love and marriage. Throughout much of history, marriage has been viewed as a means of building political and economic strength through the uniting of families and nations—as a relationship in which love is irrelevant. It has sometimes been viewed in the church as a less spiritual alternative to celibacy, while in our own day "love" is often viewed as sufficient reason for sexual activity without reference to God's design for marriage and its exclusive relationship. The book's wise teaching on love and marriage is therefore profoundly relevant for all people; it challenges every culture in a different way. We have all fallen short of God's design for our sexuality in one way or another.

At the same time, any book about marriage also has much to teach us about our relationship with Christ. Marriage itself has the primary purpose of teaching us about the relationship between Christ and the church (see Eph. 5:22–32), and as the Song convicts each of us regarding our failures in the area of sexuality, it points us to the perfect purity of our righteous husband, Jesus Christ. Christians who see Jesus in the Song of Songs by way of allegory are thus not entirely wrong, although sometimes their specific interpretations may be forced. It is unlikely that the sachet of myrrh between the woman's two breasts in Song 1:13 was originally intended to refer to Christ's coming between the two Testaments, Old and New, for example. Yet Christ is indeed to be found on every page of the Song of Songs, just as he is throughout the rest of the Scriptures.

The **author** of the book is unknown. On the basis of the superscription in 1:1, many have thought it to be written by Solomon about himself and his wife, but that interpretation misses the difference in form between the superscription of the Song and other similar superscriptions that *do* ascribe authorship to Solomon—such as Psalm 127:1. A more accurate translation of Song 1:1 is "The finest of songs: about what is Solomon's"—and, therefore, about what is *not* Solomon's as well. Solomon can hardly be presented as the ideal model of one-man/one-woman exclusive marital faithfulness, given his own acquisition of one thousand wives and concubines (see 1 Kings 11:3). Indeed, for all his money and power, Solomon doesn't understand true love at all. As depicted in the Song, Solomon's wedding day is all about himself (Song 3:6–11), which places it in complete contrast to the mutual joyful self-giving that is the theme of the Song. Solomon may be the owner of a vineyard at a place called "Husband of a multitude" (or *Baal-hamon*—8:11) that brings him a thousand shekels—a shekel for each one of his wives and concubines—but his vineyard is managed for him by others (see v. 11). In contrast, the woman is free to manage her own vineyard and to give it to the one she loves (see v. 12); her affections cannot be bought for any price (see v. 7).

An attribution of authorship to someone other than Solomon does not require the assumption made by some commentators that the woman in the Song is part of Solomon's harem while also engaging in a relationship with her shepherd-boy lover; that view creates significant moral questions about her behavior and is entirely unnecessary. It is sufficient that, as in 1 Kings 11, Solomon represents a way of approaching marriage as a means to achieve political and economic success, without reference to love. The

Song's teaching is diametrically opposite to this approach: true love cannot be purchased and is of immeasurable value (see Song 8:7), and it delights to give itself self-sacrificially in marriage, as we see when the man and the woman joyfully leave, cleave, and become one flesh (cf. Gen. 2:24).

The **structure** of the book is built around the wedding ceremony and the consummation of the lovers' relationship, which take place in 3:6–5:1 and give focus to the book's **themes**. Prior to the wedding, the lovers anticipate with eagerness the "house" (i.e., the family) they will build (see Song 1:16–17), but they know that they need to wait for the appointed time before engaging in sex. Waiting is a very important theme within the first part of the Song (see 2:8–17), and the repeated refrain that is addressed to other young women (the "daughters of Jerusalem") adjures them sternly not to stir up or awaken love until it pleases (see 2:7; 5:8; 8:4). The crucial event that is being awaited is marriage, which is the necessary context in which the God-given power of our sexuality may be unleashed safely. From its opening lines, the Song declares the goodness of God's gift of sex within marriage. The book begins with the woman longing for the man to kiss her—not simply to speak to her or lead her in a Bible study (1:2–3). She longs for the day when she will lie next to him and enjoy his caresses (2:5–6). The lovers delight in describing each other's beautiful bodies—not merely their eternal souls (5:10–16; 7:1–9). The Song affirms the appropriateness of the desire that both men and women have for sex within marriage. Sex is a good gift that God has designed to bless and strengthen our marriages.

Yet at the same time, the Song is not primarily about sex. It is actually very restrained in its descriptions of sex and uses beautiful poetic imagery to paint an impressionist rather than a realist portrait. The book is much more centrally about passion—the "Oh my goodness; I'm crazy about you" dimension of love (see Song 1:15–2:4). This is all the more remarkable given the virtually complete absence of descriptions of such emotions in the marriages that appear in the Old Testament. Many marriages fill the pages of Scripture, some good and some bad, but none of them embody more than a glimpse of the flashing fire of the love described in the Song (8:6)—with one exception: the Lord's all-encompassing love for his bride, Israel. Israel was very far from being the perfect spouse; on the contrary, she was repeatedly unfaithful to the Lord. Yet, as the story of Hosea reminds us, the Lord pursued Israel and bought her back from her lovers (see Hos. 1–3).

Only the truly fiery, passionate love that God has for us accounts for our salvation. God pursued us to the point of his own Son's death on a cross, when he bore the weight of all our sins, so that he might present us to himself as a spotless bride on the last day (see Rev. 21:2). By doing so, God has not merely given us an example of love for us to follow in our own marriages (as we see in Ephesians 5:25–28); he has himself atoned for our many failures to love in this way. His perfect desire for his bride is now credited to us, no matter what our own history of sexual and marital unfaithfulness may be, and we are loved by him just as we are. As a result, we are given the courage to try again to love our spouses in the way he has taught us and are freed from the guilt and shame that so easily holds us captive. In this way, as it guides us to behave wisely in our relationships and convicts us of our failures to live wisely in this world, the Song always points us to the Christ who is our perfect wisdom, righteousness, and strength. His unparalleled love for us is all our hope and glory.

OUTLINE

1. Title (1:1)
2. Prologue (1:2–2:7)
    - A. Introduction (1:2–14)
        - i. Desire (1:2–4)
        - ii. Uncertainty and Request (1:5–7)
        - iii. Response and Reassurance (1:8–11)
        - iv. Desire (1:12–14)
    - B. A litany of love (1:15–2:7)
        - i. Mutual Affirmation (1:15–2:3)
        - ii. The Delights and Dangers of Love (2:4–7)
3. Before the Wedding: Joined and Separated (2:8–3:5)
    - A. Morning (2:8–17)
    - B. Night (3:1–5)
4. The Wedding (3:6–5:1)
    - A. Question (3:6)
    - B. Solomon's Glory (3:7–11)

    C. The Beloved's Glory (4:1–7)
    D. Consummation (4:8–5:1)
5. After the Wedding: Separated and Rejoined (5:2–6:3)
    A. Night (5:2–8)
    B. The Lover's Glory (5:9–16)
    C. Restoration (6:1–3)
6. Contemplation and Renewed Consummation (6:4–8:4)
    A. Contemplation of the Beloved (6:4–10)
    B. Response (6:11–12)
    C. Contemplation of the Beloved (6:13–7:10a)
    D. Response (7:10b–11)
    E. Renewed Consummation (7:12–8:4)
7. Epilogue (8:5–14)
    A. The Overwhelming Power of Love (8:5–7)
    B. The Incomparable Value of Love (8:8–12)
    C. The Unending Nature of Love (8:13–14)

Iain M. Duguid
Coeditor of the Reformed Expository Commentary series
Coeditor of the Reformed Expository Bible Study series
Author of *Song of Songs* (REC)

LESSON 1

APPROACHING THE SONG OF SONGS

Song of Songs 1:1–2:7; 4:1–16; 5:2–8

THE BIG PICTURE

For centuries, the Song of Songs has both fascinated and baffled students of Scripture. Some scholars—perhaps almost embarrassed by its unabashed celebration of erotic and romantic love—have veered quickly into purely allegorical interpretations and concluded that the contents of this book must be interpreted spiritually as pertaining to Christ and the church. In more recent years, there has been a correction to this, as biblical scholars have begun to acknowledge a more objective and literal approach; such scholars have emphasized the way that the Song of Songs boldly and frankly puts love on display as something to be celebrated, enjoyed, and passionately embraced—in the context of marriage, of course.

Our study will seek to bring out the best of both these approaches; we will seek to learn from this book's positive presentation of human sexuality, romantic love, and marital bliss as being good gifts from a loving creator God. Yet as we do, we will see how this celebration of love honestly illustrates the finite nature of human love and is meant to point past it to the deeper love of a gracious God for his people—a love that went to sacrificial depths through the redeeming work of Jesus Christ. As we follow Iain Duguid's interpretation and commentary, we will assume his conclusion that the author of the book is unknown to us and will thus refer to it as the "Song of Songs" rather than the "Song of Solomon." This study will celebrate the poetic composition and arrangement of this marvelous literary work, as it moves sequentially through the book and seeks to take it at face value, while also studying it in the broader context of Scripture—the focal point of which is God's redemptive work on behalf of sinners through Christ the Son.

In this lesson, we'll take an initial big-picture look at some representative passages from the Song of Songs.

Read Song of Songs 1:1–2:7; 4:1–16; 5:2–8.

GETTING STARTED

1. Have you ever heard teaching or preaching from the Song of Songs in a church context or read study materials about this book? If so, what insights have you gleaned about it in the past? What questions do you still have about this book? Is there anything about it that confuses you?

2. What are some lies about sexual intimacy that are propagated in your culture today? Why are these lies harmful? Why is sex—and sexual sin—so powerful . . . and such an important area of life for Christians to consider carefully and biblically?

Song of Songs, pg. xx
I take the Song of Songs to be a poem by an unknown and anonymous author about two idealized people, a man and a woman, whose exclusive and committed love is great but, like all loves in this fallen world, far from perfect.

OBSERVING THE TEXT

3. As you read through the passages from Song of Songs 1, 2, and 4, what details struck you about the mood and focus of the speakers in them? What are they celebrating—and why?

4. How is human love elevated in the passages you read? What warnings are offered in them? What parts of the passages discuss potential pain and heartbreak in a relationship?

5. What seems to be the overall context of the Song of Songs? Who are the main characters? What other characters seem to be present in some of the poetry, dialogue, and songs?

UNDERSTANDING THE TEXT

6. How does the opening passage (1:1–2:7) make it clear that it's celebrating the mutuality of love between a man and a woman? In what ways do others participate in this celebration of romantic love and lend their support to it?

7. What indication does 2:7 give that romantic love must be enjoyed in the proper time, context, and way? Why is it important for us to understand that *marital* love and sexual enjoyment is what the Song of Songs celebrates?

8. What does the book's celebration of romantic, marital, and sexual love begin to teach us about the heart of our God? What do we learn about his intention for human marriage and about the good gifts he gives to human beings as their gracious Creator?

9. What seems to be happening in 4:1–16? Why might this passage make some readers and students of the Bible uncomfortable? What lessons should we learn from the fact that this passage is included in Scripture?

10. How does Song of Songs 5:2–8 remind us that even the best of human love may involve pain—and will ultimately fall short of God's perfect love?

11. In what initial ways does this book suggest that the love of Jesus the Savior is the greatest and most fulfilling love? In what ways does even the best human love fall short of God's perfect love?

Celebrating a Great Mystery, pg. xviii

[We should] recognize the Song of Songs as wisdom literature that celebrates a great mystery in life, the mutual love of a man and a woman . . . , yet that in this celebration will not only shape our thinking about human relationships but also show us profound insights into the love that Christ has for his bride, the church.

BIBLE CONNECTIONS

12. Read Proverbs 5:18–20, and note the encouragement it offers to a young man to enjoy his wife solely—and to resist the temptation to look elsewhere for sexual pleasure. From what you have read so far, how does the Song of Songs also express and teach this important command (and warning)?

13. In John's vision of the end, he sees God's people finally gathered to him in a perfected relationship. Take a moment to read Revelation 21:1–3. What main image is used to describe God's people as they are presented to him? What should this teach us about the greater reality toward which human marriage and love ought to point us?

THEOLOGY CONNECTIONS

14. As mentioned earlier, the interpretive history of the Song of Songs has involved sharp disputes and extreme disagreements in the Christian church (the story goes that John Calvin once expelled a young man from Geneva due to his interpretation of this book!). Why is it important to learn from the Song of Songs about human love, marriage, and sexual intimacy while *also* seeing that its celebratory joy is ultimately

fulfilled in the relationship between Jesus Christ and his people? How do you think that taking this approach to the book might help you as you study it?

15. According to answer 71 of the Westminster Shorter Catechism, the prohibition against adultery contained in the Ten Commandments "requires the preservation of our own and our neighbor's chastity, in heart, speech, and behavior." In what way do you think the Song of Songs is able to preserve "chastity" even as it openly and boldly celebrates sexual love, joy, and satisfaction?

APPLYING THE TEXT

16. From the passages you have read today, what applications could you begin to draw about the beauty and blessing of love that occurs within the context of marriage? Why do these passages show us that we should understand marriage to be a good and blessed gift from our creator God?

17. What warnings emerge within the passages you have read for this lesson? Why should we understand human sexuality and romantic love as being not only a great blessing but also an area for great caution and godly wisdom?

18. How is this book beginning to remind you of the ultimate fulfillment you have in Jesus Christ—your Savior and great Bridegroom? In what ways can the best human relationships illustrate for us the realities of the gospel of Jesus Christ?

PRAYER PROMPT

As you prepare for more in-depth study of the Song of Songs in the coming lessons, begin your prayer today by thanking God for the gift of this wonderful collection of poetry. Praise him for the good gift of human love, which is so unashamedly celebrated here in his Word. Praise him for the great love that he has shown to sinners through the sacrificial death of Jesus the Son. Ask him for the wisdom to learn from this book—through both its practical teaching and its gospel hints and reminders!

One Perfect Love, pg. xx

The Song is designed to show each of us how far short of perfection we fall, both as humans and as lovers, and to drive us into the arms of our true heavenly Husband, Jesus Christ, whose love for his bride is truly perfect.

LESSON 2

DESIRE AND SATISFACTION

Song of Songs 1:1–4

THE BIG PICTURE

As this lesson now begins our careful study of the Song of Songs, the text immediately plunges us into a young woman's exclamations of deep desire—with essentially no introductory comments, except to announce the title of the book (1:1). The woman boldly proclaims her desire to be covered in the "kisses" of her beloved, and she celebrates the sweetness of his love (1:2). Yet it is not only physical attraction that she celebrates; she also delights in his "name"—probably referring to his character, integrity, and reputation—which causes him to be admired by all the young women of the area (1:3). Her desire is clear: she wants to be swept away by her beloved—she wants to marry this man (1:4)!

Then, in the midst of these exclamations of desire, the "chorus" contributes for the first time, adding its own celebration of this loving relationship. This will be a continuing theme in the Song: the surrounding community has a role in celebrating marital love and encouraging a marital relationship between a man and a woman. The young woman then exclaims, one final time, "Rightly do they love you" (v. 4)[1]—again affirming the worthiness of the man to whom she longs to give her heart.

1. Different translations of the Song of Songs divide this verse in different ways and attribute it to different speakers. We follow Iain Duguid's interpretation of it, here.

As we go forward, you may notice other parts of the Song of Songs that are also organized, attributed, and labeled in different ways across different translations (including the ESV and Iain Duguid's translation).

While these opening verses show us the good and beautiful way that God has designed love and marriage between a man and a woman, they also show us the power of sexual desire. Whether this desire is fulfilled, in marriage, or left unfulfilled, we are meant to have our *deepest* longings fulfilled in Jesus Christ—our Redeemer and the lover of our souls.

Read Song of Songs 1:1–4.

GETTING STARTED

1. Have you ever had a deep desire (for an experience, a person, or an opportunity) be fulfilled? If so, what made that satisfying?

2. What is painful about longings or desires that are left unfulfilled? How has God used the pain of unfulfilled desires in your life to grow your faith and dependence on him?

A Breathless Start, pg. 4

The Song of Songs . . . plunges right into its subject matter without introducing the characters, setting the stage, or anything else, with the breathless declaration of the woman: "Oh, that he would kiss me with the kisses of his mouth!" (Song 1:2). Like love itself, the Song of Songs catches us in the midst of life and steals our breath away.

OBSERVING THE TEXT

3. Notice the way that the Song of Songs begins. Why do you think the writer simply plunges right into the poetry rather than offering an extended introduction?

4. How would you characterize the main theme and topic of these opening verses—and particularly of the woman's words about her beloved?

5. What roles do the different speakers in these opening verses play? What do these characters begin to tell you about the context of this book?

UNDERSTANDING THE TEXT

6. What makes it immediately clear that these opening verses have physical, sexual, and romantic desire in view (1:2)? Does anything surprise you about how boldly the young woman expresses her desire for her beloved? Why or why not?

7. What does she go on to say, in 1:3, that tells us her desire and love for this man are about more than simply physical attraction? What does she value about him?

8. What do you notice about the woman's invitation at the beginning of 1:4? What is her ultimate hope for this relationship?

9. What do the woman's words in 1:1–4 teach us about a right biblical view of gender? How is this woman demonstrating strength and initiative? What does she acknowledge about the role played by the man whom she loves?

Desire from Beginning to End, pg. 4

The Song of Songs is not primarily a book about sex, or a manual of dating tips, or an "agony aunt" column of relationship advice. It is a book about desire from beginning to end—desire stirred, desire frustrated, desire satisfied, desire frustrated again—but above all, desire. The woman wants something—or rather someone—with a passionate and breathless desire.

10. As the plural voices of the chorus speak up, what do they offer to this first scene? In what way do they affirm love, desire, and romance? What might this be meant to teach the reader?

11. What does the passionate and intense romantic desire that we see in these opening verses tell us about the desire we should have for Jesus Christ, our true bridegroom? How can unfulfilled desire (as well as sexual desire that is fulfilled within marriage) draw us to find satisfaction in our Savior?

BIBLE CONNECTIONS

12. Read God's warning to Cain in Genesis 4:7. How does this passage make it clear that desire is not always pure and good? Why must Christians discern between good and rightly ordered desires and desires that are motivated by sin and must be put to death?

13. In 1 Corinthians 7:1–5, the apostle Paul lays out some principles regarding sexual intimacy in marriage and explains a husband and

wife's mutual "ownership" of each other. What does Paul tell us about the connection between marriage and the fulfillment of sexual desire? What central principles and truths guide his practical instructions?

THEOLOGY CONNECTIONS

14. In his commentary, Iain Duguid refers to Augustine's well-known words "You have made our hearts for yourself, O Lord, and our hearts are restless until they find repose in you."[2] How does this lesson's passage reveal the "restless" heart of a lover who desires her beloved? Why must followers of Jesus never allow romantic love to become an end in itself—or an idol?

15. According to the Westminster Confession of Faith, marriage was "ordained for the mutual help of husband and wife" (24.2). Where do we see evidence of this purpose for marriage in the passage for this lesson?

2. Augustine, *Confessions*, trans. E. B. Pusey (New York: E. P. Dutton & Co., 1949), 1.1 (language updated); quoted in Iain M. Duguid, *Song of Songs*, Reformed Expository Commentary (Phillipsburg, NJ: P&R Publishing, 2016), 10.

APPLYING THE TEXT

16. What can these opening verses teach us about the goodness of sexual and romantic desire—when it is rightly ordered in the context of marriage between a man and a woman? How do these verses affirm such desire?

17. What do we see in this passage to indicate that the man and woman are different and distinct from each other? What might this be telling us about God's intentions regarding gender and marriage?

18. What light can this passage shed on the gospel of Jesus Christ—and particularly on the relationship between that gospel and the deepest desires of our hearts? What should this passage lead us to confess? What ought it to teach us to seek above all else?

A Call to Relationship, pg. 10

The Song of Songs calls us to a relationship with the One who entered this world of disordered desires and loved perfectly in our place. Jesus Christ is truly the One whose name is above all names. The aroma of Christ and his righteousness fills the world with true sweetness and beauty (2 Cor. 2:14); as Christians, we are all longing for the day when he will come and sweep us off our feet and carry us off to our heavenly home so that our relationship can finally be fulfilled.

PRAYER PROMPT

As you close your study of this first passage from the Song of Songs, ask God to rightly order your deepest desires—and to make Jesus Christ, his Son, their main object! Our sexual desires, when fulfilled in marriage, are meant to spur us to pursue our true Bridegroom. Desires that are unfulfilled in this life are meant to drive us toward Christ, the love of our souls, as well. Pray that God would help you to truly delight in Christ, above all, so that you can find eternal satisfaction in him.

LESSON 3

AFFIRMATION AND INTIMACY

Song of Songs 1:5–14

THE BIG PICTURE

As the poetic love story of the Song of Songs continues, the young woman's speech becomes a dialogue as the man she loves responds to her. The passage begins with questions and insecurity; the woman is hesitant about her humble status when she compares herself with the other women of her area (1:5–6). In addition, the man she loves is poetically portrayed here as a shepherd—someone on the move and often gone—which makes her wonder not only if he will accept her but even if she will be able to find him (1:7).

The man responds, though, with heartwarming affirmation and loving desire, assuring the young woman of his commitment and devotion and even offering directions so that she can find him (1:8). He then answers her expressions of admiration with some of his own, praising her beauty and affirming his attraction to her and desire for her (1:9–10). The woman's questions are answered; her insecurities about her appearance and her difficulty with finding her beloved are laid to rest by this man who is ready to affirm, praise, and commit to her.

As the "chorus" of surrounding friends again declare their affirmation of this loving relationship (1:11), the woman responds with renewed admiration of the man she loves, using evocative language of spices and perfume to describe the intimacy and delight of their desire, attraction, and romance (1:12–14). We, as readers, are meant to be delighted in the mutual commitment of these lovers as they offer affirmation to each other. Even so, we are again pointed beyond this romance to an intimacy far deeper than the best human marriage. The Savior of our souls has sought us out, affirmed his love for us at the cross, and committed himself completely to our eternal joy and security.

Read Song of Songs 1:5–14.

GETTING STARTED

1. Have you struggled with insecurity in your relationships with the opposite sex? If you are married, what makes it so important for you to feel secure in and affirmed by the love and admiration of your spouse? What goes wrong when insecurity creeps into a loving marriage relationship?

2. What signs might indicate that someone has made human intimacy an idol? What can we be tempted to demand, from human intimacy, that only God can provide?

Pursuing Intimacy with God, pg. 13

As wisdom literature, this passage provides us with guidance and encouragement from God that will challenge, convict, and direct us as we pursue our own romantic relationships. Yet the greatest love story of all—the true Song of Songs in our lives—is our relationship with the God who made us for himself. As a result, this passage also speaks to our relationship with God and our pursuit of intimacy with him.

OBSERVING THE TEXT

3. In the opening verses of this passage (1:5–7), what tone does the young woman seem to have? What makes her self-conscious? What causes her to question the relationship and commitment of the man she loves?

4. What answer does the man give to her questions, and how does he put her concerns to rest, in 1:8–10? How can these verses encourage and bring joy to the reader of the Song of Songs?

5. What is the woman's tone as she responds to the man's affirmation (1:12–14)? What note does the passage end on, in contrast to how it began?

UNDERSTANDING THE TEXT

6. It is important to understand that when the woman describes herself as "dark," she is referring not to an ethnic feature but to a class and status feature—most likely one that ties her to the working class of people

who labor under the hot sun (1:5–6). Why might this be making the woman self-conscious about her status with the man she loves?

7. What might be implied by the fact that the woman mentions her mother—but not her father (1:6)? What does 1:7 imply about her beloved's profession? What questions does she raise in this verse—and what does she articulate about the struggle and confusion she is experiencing?

8. What assurance and affirmation does the man offer as he responds to the woman (1:8)? How, specifically, does he answer her concerns about finding him?

9. What does the man then go on to do in 1:9–10—and what makes this another moment of affirmation and assurance for the young woman?

10. As the "chorus" again contributes its voice of approval and admiration for this loving relationship, the woman sings the praises of her beloved man (1:12–14). What does she affirm about him? How does she again express her love and desire—and, this time, with renewed confidence?

11. What do we learn from this passage about the beauty of security, affirmation, and mutual admiration in the context of a marriage relationship? What does this passage teach us about our relationship with our Savior, who loves and cherishes us unconditionally?

BIBLE CONNECTIONS

12. Read Genesis 2:18–23. How does God affirm the goodness of the coming together of a man and a woman through marriage? How does Adam respond? What can we learn about God—and about human marriage—from this foundational text?

Made for Intimacy, pg. 20

The Bible tells us that it is not good for a man to be alone (Gen. 2:18), and the same is true for women as well. We were not made to live alone but to pursue intimacy with one another. Although God has given some people the gift of singleness as a vocation, most people are called to find their deepest intimacy through the relationship of marriage.

13. In Psalm 16, which ends in verse 11 with an anticipation of "pleasures forevermore" at God's right hand, David also declares to God, "I have no good apart from you" (v. 2). What does it mean for followers of Jesus to embrace this mindset? In what ways are our marriages and friendships strengthened when we make God our ultimate good and greatest satisfaction?

THEOLOGY CONNECTIONS

14. Answer 20 of the Westminster Larger Catechism explains that God blessed man at the time of his creation by "ordaining marriage for his help [and] affording him communion with himself." How do these two great gifts of God work together? What happens when we pursue marriage for our "help" without also passionately pursuing "communion" with our God?

15. As we continue to study the Song of Songs, we will see the tension between rightly *honoring* marriage and *idolizing* it. What signs in someone's life might hint that intimacy or romantic love—good gifts from God for marriage—are becoming idolized rather than simply honored?

APPLYING THE TEXT

16. What can you learn from this passage about healthy affirmation, admiration, and mutual love and respect in a marriage? Why are these things important to a marriage?

17. How does the hope of the gospel affirm, comfort, and encourage you? What has Jesus done to make himself easy for sinners to find when they need him and seek him?

18. In what ways do you perhaps seek too much from the meaningful human relationships in your life? Do you have trouble believing that ultimately satisfying intimacy comes only through your relationship with your Savior, Jesus Christ? Why or why not?

True Intimacy, pg. 23

Even the church will often let us down and disappoint us. Even in the best marriage and the best church, our longings for sexual and relational intimacy never find complete fulfillment in this broken world. The richest and deepest hope of intimacy is not to be found in any merely human relationship. . . . True intimacy is ultimately to be found only in the One who loved us before the world began, Jesus Christ.

PRAYER PROMPT

As you close your study of this reassuring exchange between the two lovers in the Song of Songs, ask God to expand your understanding of the deep love he has shown for you in Christ the Son. Thank him for not only opening his arms so that you could find him but also acting to seek and save lost sinners such as you! Praise him for the grace and mercy he has shown by accepting you as you are—and forgiving you completely through the cleansing blood Jesus shed on the cross. Ask God for strength to value intimacy with him above all human intimacy, even as you pursue healthy intimacy and affirmation within your relationships.

LESSON 4

CRAZY LOVE

Song of Songs 1:15–2:7

THE BIG PICTURE

Within the renewed security and confidence of mutual love, the man and woman's romance deepens—and becomes even more intimate—in the passage we will study in this lesson. The man and woman express their love, desire, and admiration for each other as they exchange words that are rich with passion and pleasure.

The passage begins with the man celebrating the beauty of the woman—and noting especially the loveliness of her eyes (1:15). She quickly responds, praising his physical appearance and then celebrating the intimacy and security within their relationship, before acknowledging with confidence her own place as his beloved one (1:16–2:1). The man then affirms the exalted place she holds among women—at least in his eyes (2:2)! Through their mutual exaltation of each other, they put the beautiful complementarity of the relationship between a man and a woman on full display here.

The woman's final response shows that her desire for intimacy is deepening (2:3–6). She describes her need for the embrace of her beloved, the sweetness of his taste, and her sense of being "sick" with love as they both wait for the consummation of their marriage (v. 5). Within this celebration of sexual desire and intimacy, though, there emerges a word of warning, as the woman turns outward to the "daughters of Jerusalem" and urges them to wait patiently for the right time and context for this kind of love (2:7). This points us to the proper context for all this intimacy, passion, desire, and delight: marriage between a man and a woman, as it is created and ordered by God. Such delight and passion, when rightly enjoyed and satisfied within marriage, continue to teach us about the even deeper intimacy and delight we can share with the Bridegroom of God's people: Jesus Christ the Lord.

Read Song of Songs 1:15–2:7.

GETTING STARTED

1. Why is there such pleasure in knowing that the love, admiration, or respect we feel for another person is *mutually shared*?

2. Why must the church continue to offer warnings about sexual sin and temptation—even as the surrounding culture mocks and disregards such warnings? In what instances have you seen Christians express these warnings well?

Passion Is Powerful, pg. 31

God has created us in such a way that love is powerful; sexual passion is powerful. It is not something to be toyed with. Yet neither is love or sex something to be denigrated or denied because it is somehow dirty or unspiritual. There is a proper time for love and sexual passion, a time when it will be appropriate and right to release its overwhelming power.

OBSERVING THE TEXT

3. How does the dialogue between the man and the woman in this passage shape our understanding of the nature of this relationship? What is the tone of the comments they make to each other—and how do they demonstrate their confidence in each other's love?

4. How does this passage make clear that its focus is sexual enjoyment and fulfillment between the man and the woman? What metaphors, word pictures, and images does it use to alert us to this?

5. How do you think the stern warning in 2:7 relates to the preceding verses (2:3–6)? What might be spurring the woman on to offer this warning to the young women of her community?

UNDERSTANDING THE TEXT

6. What words does the man repeat in the opening verse of this passage (1:15)? What makes them into words of affirmation and assurance—especially in light of the passage we studied in our last lesson?

7. While the woman compliments the physical appearance of the man as well, in the first part of 1:16, she quickly turns to celebrating the intimacy and delight of their relationship. How does she do this, in the rest of that verse and the next? What does she then assert about herself—and what might this be demonstrating about the way she views herself (2:1)?

8. How does the man communicate his committed and devoted love for this *one* particular woman (2:2)? What makes an assertion and commitment like this so important to a godly marriage?

9. What images, words, and metaphors make it clear to us that sexual love and intimacy are the focus of 2:3–6? What aspects of the relationship she desires with her husband does the woman celebrate?

10. As the woman suddenly turns outward to speak in verse 7 to the "daughters of Jerusalem," what specific warning does she offer them? What makes this warning so important? Why do you think her passion in 2:3–6 prompts this warning?

11. This passage unashamedly celebrates marital love and sexual intimacy. What does that teach us about the Bible's view of human sexuality? In what ways should even this "bedroom scene" drive us to see our need for an even greater intimacy with our Savior and true Bridegroom?

BIBLE CONNECTIONS

12. Proverbs 5:15–19 contains echoes of both the marital delight and the warnings we have seen in this passage we are studying. Read those verses now. What stern warnings does the passage offer against sexual sin? How does it celebrate and affirm sexual delight within the context of marriage?

13. Images of feasting and fruit dominate the most sexually explicit verses within this passage from the Song of Songs (apple trees, fruit, a banquet, raisins). Take a moment to read Revelation 22:1–5, and note its images of water, trees, and fruit. How can this vision of the new heaven and new earth serve to remind us that the best "feasts" on earth are only a hint of the pleasure and satisfaction that are to come?

Mutual Affirmation and Respect, pg. 29

Each has affirming words to say about the other, building the other person up rather than tearing down. . . . This pattern of mutual affirmation and respect is tremendously important in a healthy marriage.

THEOLOGY CONNECTIONS

14. According to answer 138 in the Westminster Larger Catechism, the "duties" required by the seventh commandment's prohibition of adultery include "chastity in body, mind, affections, words, and behavior; and the preservation of it in ourselves and others; watchfulness over the eyes and all the senses; temperance, keeping of chaste company, modesty in apparel; marriage by those that have not the gift of continency, conjugal love, and cohabitation; diligent labor in our callings; shunning all occasions of uncleanness, and resisting temptations thereunto." How do we infer these same duties from the positive picture that Song of Songs 2:3–6 paints of sexual intimacy, as well as from the warning contained in 2:7?

15. Jesus taught that marriage will be no more in the new heaven and new earth (see Matt. 22:30). If marriage is for this age only and not for the age to come, how does that impact our perspective on its purpose? What does earthly marriage prepare us for and anticipate?

Sanctified Uniquely, pg. 35

God sanctifies each of his children in a unique way, giving each of them his or her own story. It is always tempting to long for the story that God wrote for someone else, whether that story is marriage, or a seemingly better marriage than ours, or even singleness. Yet God wrote your personal story with the goal of sanctifying you in exactly the ways he planned.

APPLYING THE TEXT

16. How should this passage encourage Christian spouses to offer each other admiration, encouragement, affirmation, and loving compliments? What is beautiful about the dialogue that we studied in this lesson's passage—and how should it guide Christians in their marriages?

17. What do we learn in this passage about the power of sexual intimacy? Why should we be diligent about guarding sexual purity, for the glory of our God, and enjoying it only in its proper context?

18. Why should the celebration of intimacy and delight in this text (and particularly in 2:3–6) strengthen our hunger and desire for more intimacy with Jesus Christ our Savior—whether we are married or single?

PRAYER PROMPT

As you respond to your study of this passage with prayer, begin by considering how God created and ordered human marriage—along with sexual intimacy, delight, and pleasure. Praise him for his creative and loving hand that created this good gift for human beings. Then ask him for strength and commitment so that you can worshipfully protect and guard this gift of sexual intimacy—even by warning others. Ask him for a deepening intimacy with your Savior—the great Bridegroom who died and rose for you and who now lives to intercede for you until you see him face-to-face.

LESSON 5

WAITING

Song of Songs 2:8–17

THE BIG PICTURE

As the man and woman continue their dialogue, one clear theme emerges: *waiting*. Both lovers voice their desire for each other while also describing the agonizing experience of patiently waiting to consummate their love.

As the woman looks forward to the day when her beloved will make her his wife (2:8–9), she pictures him "leaping" and rushing toward her. The man responds with an invitation for her to "come away"—most likely a reference to her departure from her childhood home so that she can join him as his wife (2:10–12). He repeats this invitation, in 2:13, with words that evoke images of sexual fulfillment and physical intimacy; the man longs to enjoy the "form" of the woman he loves (2:14 TOTC)! But the young woman's final words in this passage slow the man down: she assures him of her love, and of her intention to belong to him, yet also urges him to wait "until the day comes to life" (2:15–17 TOTC). Here is a couple who are deeply in love—and yet are waiting patiently until the day of their wedding for the full consummation and expression of their love for each other.

As with previous passages, the careful student of Scripture can find layers of interpretation and application here. This passage reminds us that God's plan and purpose for sexual fulfillment unfold *only* in the context of marriage between one man and one woman. Christians do well to wait—patiently—for that God-ordained context for sexual intimacy. And the broader theme of waiting also reminds us that all Christians are called to wait—patiently and sometimes agonizingly—for the day that is coming when we will finally be in the presence of Jesus. Married or single, we all wait for a day when we will be free from sin, sickness, pain, and grief—as well as free to enjoy fellowship and intimacy with the great Lover of our souls.

Read Song of Songs 2:8–17.

GETTING STARTED

1. Why is waiting for the fulfillment of a desire sometimes agonizing? When have you experienced the almost unbearable *ache* of waiting for something or someone?

2. Describe a time you have enjoyed something in its right time or place. What can go wrong when a person attempts to enjoy a good thing in the *wrong* context?

Waiting Is Not Forever, pg. 53
We wait. But waiting is not forever. So wait with patience for that great day, when your hopes will finally be fulfilled. Look forward to your wedding feast that is yet to come, when all of life's disappointments and failures will be past, and we will joyfully drink the wedding cup of the new covenant in heaven, with Jesus.

OBSERVING THE TEXT

3. Again, in this passage, we see a dialogue between a man and a woman who love each other deeply but are waiting for the full consummation of their love that sexual intimacy will provide. How do they both affirm and guide each other?

4. What particular role does the woman seem to play, in this passage, as she responds to the intense desire of the man? What does she do to caution him, even as she assures him of her love?

5. What does this passage celebrate? What implicit warnings does it contain regarding the pursuit of sexual intimacy and desire at the wrong time or in the wrong context?

UNDERSTANDING THE TEXT

6. What does the woman picture her beloved doing as this passage opens (2:8–9)? What does the way that she pictures him imply about how he feels about her—and what can we learn about her own feelings?

7. What does the opening of the man's speech to his beloved suggest that its main theme will be (2:10)? What does this invitation reveal about his feelings for her?

8. What images from nature does the man incorporate in 2:12–13 to describe the beauty of love and his readiness for sexual intimacy with the woman he loves? What makes these images sexually evocative?

9. What invitation does the man again repeat near the end of 2:13—and how does he express his desire for his beloved, and his physical attraction to her, in 2:14?

10. As the woman slows the man down and reminds him to wait, what might she mean when she tells him about catching the "foxes" in the vineyard (2:15)?

11. Even while she urges her beloved to continue to wait patiently, what assurance does the woman again give him of her love and desire for

him (2:16–17)? How can what she says apply to our own experience of waiting for the day of resurrection and our perfected relationship with our Savior?

BIBLE CONNECTIONS

12. Second Samuel 13:1–19 describes the horror and evil of sexual desire that is detached from love, patience, and self-restraint. Skim through this devastating passage. In what ways do you see sexual desire going wrong in this account? What warnings does this passage contain?

13. Read 1 Peter 5:10–11. How does Peter comfort the suffering "elect exiles" (1 Peter 1:1) of God? What do these verses say God's people should be waiting for expectantly?

The Time Is Not Yet Right, pg. 45
She, too, longs for the day when the wall will come down and all barriers between them are gone, so that she can fully be his and he can fully be hers forever. Yet in spite of that ongoing, aching desire, she acknowledges that the time is not yet right. Until the day comes to life and the shadows flee away—that is, until the morning has fully come—he will have to leave alone.

THEOLOGY CONNECTIONS

14. According to answer 71 of the Westminster Shorter Catechism, the seventh commandment "requires the preservation of our own, and our neighbor's chastity, in heart, speech, and behavior." How does the woman obey this commandment in the passage we have just studied?

15. God's Word does not promise that all our desires will be fulfilled perfectly during this life. How can this passage—through its focus on desires that are present while also being presently unfulfilled—shape our understanding of how to live faithfully in the midst of unfulfilled desires? Why is faithfulness to Jesus in times of waiting such an important part of Christian discipleship?

Don't Stay Away, pg. 52

Have you heard and responded to his invitation? Can you say today of Jesus, "My beloved is mine and I am his, forever and forever"? Today, he calls you to come and lay down your heart before him. Don't let your sin and brokenness keep you away—he died to pay for each of those sins. Don't let your own attempts at goodness keep you away. . . . Come to the Beloved who calls to you, "Arise, my darling, my beautiful one, and come away."

APPLYING THE TEXT

16. What does this text have to teach single Christians who desire marriage and sexual intimacy? How can the passage serve to guide Christian couples while they are dating and engaged?

17. What do we learn about the power of sex from this passage? Why must sexual intimacy be carefully guarded, protected, and enjoyed within the bounds of its God-ordained context?

18. How can this passage encourage you as you wait to be freed from sin and to experience the final redemption of your body? In what way can even desires that are left unfulfilled in this life deepen your love for Jesus and your expectation of heaven?

PRAYER PROMPT

As you reflect on this lesson's passage, pray that God would strengthen you to be able to protect and guard his gift of sexual intimacy—whether you are married, single, widowed, or otherwise waiting. Ask for his help with strengthening your own patience and for his wisdom to shape the guidance and counsel you give to others about sexual temptation and desire. Most importantly, pray that God would remind you that the Christian life always involves waiting. Pray that your hope will be rightly ordered as you look forward to the coming day of resurrection joy and the fellowship you will experience in the presence of the Lord Jesus!

LESSON 6

SEARCHING

Song of Songs 3:1–5

THE BIG PICTURE

As the third chapter of the Song of Songs begins, we come to an extended speech given by the woman. Her tone has shifted, and the scene has changed: she is no longer in the presence of her beloved or speaking directly to him but is describing her frustrating and frantic search for him. The reader is invited to relate to her pain and to her search for intimacy and security.

The search that the woman describes in this passage is dreamlike; the beginning of verse 1 tells us that this restless search takes place as she lies on her "bed night after night" (3:1 TOTC). She paces the city and asks everyone where he might be—yet remains unable to track him down (3:2–3). Finally, she finds this man she loves and seizes him passionately as she is filled with a longing to share married bliss with him in her family chambers (3:4). After this passionate climax to her frantic search, she again urges the young women of Jerusalem to wait—and not to "awaken" love until it "delights" (3:5 TOTC).

This passage captures not only the search for love and intimacy that we all know but also the moment when love is found. It is good to pursue love in its proper context—and many people will find satisfaction in the marriage God has ordained for them. But our ultimate search for intimacy and satisfaction will never reach its final fulfillment except through the God who made us. Our restless searching, longing, and seeking has an eternal goal: the everlasting joy available through Jesus our Savior.

Read Song of Songs 3:1–5.

GETTING STARTED

1. How would you say that restlessness and dissatisfaction characterize the lives of people in your culture or community? What are people seeking? How do they try to find fulfillment, joy, belonging, and satisfaction?

2. Given our desire for intimacy—and particularly for sexual and romantic intimacy—what dangers and temptations must we keep in mind? How can a good desire for intimacy lead us to make sinful and short-sighted attempts to find satisfaction?

The Joyful Conclusion, pg. 55
As this passage in the Song of Songs reminds us, as well as being dizzying and dazzling, love is often painful, frustrating, and confusing, as we search for a deep intimacy that keeps escaping us. That is true both in our human relationships and in our search for God. . . . Therefore, as we examine the frustrating side of the search for intimacy, we will think about why we should keep on searching for love in the midst of its challenges, as well as of the ultimate joyful conclusion to that search.

OBSERVING THE TEXT

3. What do you observe about the woman's tone in the first three verses of this passage? What seems to be her state of mind? What worries her—and what does she seek?

4. How are the woman's desires satisfied—and what is the conclusion to her frantic search? What does she ultimately seem to be after?

5. After the woman's description of her dreamlike search and internal struggle, how does the tone of the text shift in 3:5? Whom does she turn to address? Why do you think she makes this abrupt shift?

Sex in the Right Context, pg. 57
We should also recognize that in her dreams this young woman doesn't simply long for sex: she longs for sex in the appropriate context—the context of home and family. . . . She wants to bring him to the house of her mother, to the very chamber where she was conceived. What she means by that is that she wants to bring the man into the epicenter of her life and her own family history.

UNDERSTANDING THE TEXT

6. How do the opening words of this chapter establish the dreamlike quality of this section? If what the woman is describing is indeed to be understood as a dreamlike, emotional struggle amid her desire for love and intimacy, what longings and insecurities might be lying beneath her restless search?

7. What fears does the woman seem to be expressing in the last two lines of 3:1? What does she ultimately seek—and what is she unable to find?

8. What position does the woman place herself in as she searches for her beloved (3:2–3)? What indications are there that her search is frantic and desperate?

9. When she finds her beloved (3:4), what does the woman do? What seems to be her goal and intention? What hints do we see in this verse of her desire for marital—and even sexual—fulfillment?

10. We find the woman issuing another word of warning and caution at the conclusion of this restless dream sequence (3:5). Why do you think this particular dream, of the woman's frantic search and loving "seizure," leads her to turn to other young women and give them this word of warning? What is she again teaching us about sexual purity and patience?

11. How does this dreamlike section capture the search for intimacy and belonging that is part of the human experience? What might it tell us about our *spiritual* pursuit and longings?

BIBLE CONNECTIONS

12. Jeremiah 2:13 speaks of the foolish tendency all human beings have to seek satisfaction in "cisterns" of our own creation rather than drinking deeply of the God who created us. Read that verse now, and note its surrounding context. In what places have you searched for satisfaction, intimacy, and delight? How might God be calling you to find deeper delight in him by placing your faith in his Son?

13. Read Luke 15:1–7 and note the shepherd's diligent search for his one lost sheep. What does this tell us about our Savior? What does our Great Shepherd do for lost sinners who are searching for meaning and satisfaction in the dark?

THEOLOGY CONNECTIONS

14. The philosopher Blaise Pascal famously spoke of a God-shaped hole, or vacuum, that exists within the heart of every human being. What can this lesson's passage contribute to your understanding of humanity's pursuit of meaning, satisfaction, and joy? In what ways does this passage picture the gospel for us?

15. The Westminster Confession of Faith explains that *effectual calling* is "of God's free and special grace alone, not from any thing at all foreseen in man; who is altogether passive therein, until, being quickened and renewed by the Holy Spirit, he is thereby enabled to answer this call, and to embrace the grace offered and conveyed in it" (10.2). In the gospel, who does the searching—and why is that such good news?

APPLYING THE TEXT

16. What does this passage tell us about our God-given longings for human intimacy—and even for sex? What attitude should we take toward the fulfillment of those longings, when it happens within marriage, and why?

17. With the woman's warning in mind, what must we remember about the power—and danger—of sexual intimacy when it is pursued in sinful ways?

18. How does this passage resonate with you, and with your own pursuit of intimacy with God and of spiritual joy and security? What would it mean for you to "seize" Christ by faith? How can you increase your satisfaction and pleasure in him?

An Invitation to Search and Be Found, pg. 64

The black darkness of our night is actually God's invitation to us to search for him—to search diligently, eagerly, longingly, as the woman in the poem searches for her man. . . . Yet the good news of the gospel is that the One for whom we search is not playing hide-and-seek with us. He, too, is searching for us.

PRAYER PROMPT

In Christ, we have an eternal Bridegroom who will never be lost to us; he has made himself known and will be found by all who repent of their sin and humbly turn to him in faith. Today, praise God that you will never know the pain of a restless search that finally and ultimately has no conclusion. Thank him that you are able to find eternal joy, comfort, and satisfaction in a Savior who stretches out scarred hands to embrace you forever. Ask your God for the strength to be able to enjoy sexual fulfillment in his ordained context (should you be called to marriage); but, even more importantly, ask him for help through his Spirit so that you can find your greatest joy in your crucified and risen Savior.

LESSON 7

MONEY CAN'T BUY LOVE

Song of Songs 3:6–4:7

THE BIG PICTURE

The emotions and desires of the two lovers have been ramping up as the Song of Songs has progressed. The man and woman have traded compliments and expressed their yearning for each other. Their passionate desire for intimacy and sexual enjoyment has been tempered by their recognition that it is wise to wait until they can fulfill these desires in a marital context. Now we reach their wedding day—a day of celebration in which they will joyfully consummate their love. And we find a curious contrast: the pomp and regality of wealth and ceremony . . . and the simple beauty and power of love that transcends a lover's status or station.

The first section of this passage (3:6–11) begins with the awe-inspiring spectacle of Solomon's glory, pomp, and wealth, which is described in bright and vivid detail. The air around this regal ruler is filled with the scent of expensive spices and perfumes (v. 6), and his wonderful bed—which is described as his "litter" or "carriage"—is guarded by "sixty mighty men" and both fashioned from and decorated with the most expensive materials on earth (vv. 7–10). Amid this pomp and glory, the king arrives in splendor for his wedding celebration (v. 11).

The next section, which begins with the same expression as the first ("Behold"), nonetheless presents a clear contrast. Gone are all displays of pomp, wealth, and ceremony. The young man simply celebrates, with love and admiration, the shape and form of the woman he loves (4:1–7). As his gaze takes in her body, shape, and appearance, he expresses his awe and appreciation of her with metaphors and word pictures that spring from his time and culture. The section concludes as he moves from talking about the physical appearance of the woman he loves to celebrating *everything* about her (v. 7). His simple, pure, strong love illustrates the love of our eternal God, whose favor is more valuable than all the wealth this world can offer.

Read Song of Songs 3:6–4:7.

GETTING STARTED

1. What temptations do you feel to place too much emphasis on money, appearance, or comfort? In what ways does entertainment, advertising, or the pressure of those around you contribute to these temptations?

2. Why do many people value, celebrate, and seek after "true love"? What are the spiritual dangers of chasing perfect romantic love?

The Simplicity of Pure Love, pg. 69

The poet is going to contrast the glory and splendor of Solomon's self-centered palace and extravagant wedding with the simplicity and purity of true love. Money may buy a splendid wedding ceremony in which the camera is focused entirely on you, but money can't buy you love.

OBSERVING THE TEXT

3. What grandiose details and descriptions of over-the-top pomp and wealth do you find in the first part of this passage (3:6–11)?

4. In what ways do the tone, and especially the focus, of the second part of this passage (4:1–7) differ from those of the first?

5. Compared to the second scene, what does the first scene lack, despite the abundance of lavish wealth it portrays? What might this contrast be meant to teach us?

UNDERSTANDING THE TEXT

6. As this passage opens, what *kind* of person is it portraying (3:6)? What immediately alerts us to his status, wealth, and power?

7. What might be the significance of the perfumes and fragrances that are mentioned in conjunction with the arrival of this king (3:6)? What do we notice about the *security* of his place of rest (3:7–8)? How do these opening verses display his self-focus, and perhaps even pride?

8. What about the description of the king's bed indicates immense (and perhaps over-the-top) wealth (3:9–10)? What is the focus of this king's wedding celebration (3:11) . . . and what seems to be missing from its description?

9. The focus of the text shifts as we see the passage's second "Behold" (4:1). What does the text now have in view? How does its new focus differ from what came before?

10. Note the different metaphors and word pictures that the man uses to describe the beauty of his beloved (4:2–6). Which of these are surprising and strange to us today? Pick at least two of these images and discuss what the man might mean by using them.

11. As this passage concludes, in 4:7, do you believe the man is referring to the woman's physical appearance alone? Why or why not? How can this entire section serve to give us a glimpse of Christ's celebration over and delight in his eternal bride, the church?

BIBLE CONNECTIONS

12. Read Hebrews 13:5. As is the case in other places in Scripture, money *itself* is not identified as being evil or sinful here; instead, what are Christians commanded to keep away from their lives? What positive promise and reminder does this verse offer as the foundation for this warning and command?

13. In Zephaniah 3:17, God delights over his people with singing. Read that verse now, and note its surrounding context. What does this verse, in combination with Song of Songs 4:1–7, tell us about God's feelings toward his redeemed people?

Where Is the Spotlight Pointing?, pg. 77
In contrast to the Solomonic model, in which the spotlight shines with undivided attention on Solomon alone, the man in the poem has his eyes entirely fixed on his spouse-to-be. . . . He shines the spotlight entirely on her and delights in who she is.

THEOLOGY CONNECTIONS

14. From the very beginning, God's intention has been for human sexual desire to be fulfilled only in the context of marriage between a man and a woman. Turn back to Genesis 2:23—the foundational passage regarding marriage—and note what Adam says about Eve. In what ways, in Song of Songs 4:1–7, does the young man echo and amplify Adam's celebratory words of affirmation ?

15. Answer 108 of the Heidelberg Catechism explains that the seventh commandment calls us to "live a chaste and continent [meaning self-restrained] life both within and outside of holy wedlock." How can the celebration of marital delight serve to promote chastity "within" marriage? What kind of restraint are Christians who are "outside of" marriage called to practice?

You Matter to God, pg. 79
The God of the universe so loved you that he sent his only Son to come into this world and die for you. You matter to him. He cares for you, even though you have not cared for him and have run from him, perhaps finding yourself today in a spiritual wilderness far from home. His gaze is nonetheless fixed on you, not just as one human being out of a teeming mass of humanity, but as an individual creation of his hands.

APPLYING THE TEXT

16. What does this passage teach us about earthly treasure and wealth? What truths about money and earthly comfort are important for you to keep in mind as you pursue deeper joy in and through Christ?

17. What can we say about the admiration that the man in this passage from the Song of Songs shows for the woman? What can this teach us about love and adoration that are located within the proper context of marriage?

18. The man tells his bride, "There is no flaw in you" (4:7). Is this something Christ can say of *his* bride, the church? Why or why not? How does this show us that Christ's delight in his people is much more marvelous and miraculous than the man's delight in the woman in this passage?

PRAYER PROMPT

Solomon's display of earthly wealth and glory pales in comparison to the simple beauty of genuine love that is openly celebrated between a man and a woman in this passage. Today, ask God to give you his perspective on money and wealth as you pray for him to enable you to see earthly treasure as he sees it. Pray that he would allow you to enjoy more deeply the love and delight for you that he has shown through Christ.

LESSON 8

CONSUMMATION

Song of Songs 4:8–5:1

THE BIG PICTURE

This passage, which falls essentially at the center of the Song of Songs, takes us to the "bedroom scene" that follows the wedding of this young man and woman who are deeply in love. The lovers have taken turns expressing their mutual desire and admiration; they have searched for and found each other; they have patiently and agonizingly waited. Now the wedding celebration has reached its climax—and the enjoyment of marital intimacy can begin.

The man's speech in this scene is full of desire and rich with evocative imagery and phrases (4:8–15). After an opening invitation to his wife, he expresses delight over her "caresses" (v. 10 TOTC) as well as over her lips and even the way she smells (v. 11). And even in the midst of their intimacy, the man again celebrates her chastity; he rejoices that she has been a "locked garden" as she has waited for sex within marriage (v. 12 TOTC). He uses images of fruit, perfume, and flowing streams to further evoke the delight of the marriage bed and its sexual fulfillment (vv. 13–15).

The woman's response is joyful, willing, and positive, showing no more restraint or caution (4:16). Within the security and commitment of marriage, she invites her husband to enjoy sexual intimacy with her. The passage concludes with four intense and sexually evocative statements by the husband—"I come," "I pluck," "I eat," "I drink" (5:1 TOTC). As the curtain closes on this bedroom scene, marital love is again joyfully celebrated and affirmed by the "daughters of Jerusalem" at the end of that same verse (TOTC). The marriage has been consummated—and even in this blissful moment, we are reminded of the greater marital bliss to which every wedding celebration points: the marriage supper of the Lamb!

Read Song of Songs 4:8–5:1.

GETTING STARTED

1. In what ways have pop culture and the entertainment industry glamorized sex? What have they done to rip it from its proper—and private—context within the marriage bed? What impact does this have on men and women?

2. Why do Christian churches sometimes hesitate to talk and teach frankly about sex and intimacy? What might we miss if we never talk about sexual intimacy in Christian circles?

Marriage and Sex, pg. 82
And so to bed. Or rather, "And so to wed." Or more precisely still, both together. This three-stanza poem at the very heart of the Song explores and extols the intimate and God-designed connection between marriage and sex.

OBSERVING THE TEXT

3. What word in 4:8 clues the reader in to the fact that the wedding is now complete—and that a *married* couple is now the focal point of the Song? How else does the man refer to the woman, and what might this language be suggesting?

4. What sexually evocative pictures, phrases, and metaphors appear throughout this passage? What physical senses are mentioned? In what way do these poetic pictures, although evocative, demonstrate a kind of prudence and modesty?

5. What do you notice about the attitudes that the man and the woman hold in this passage toward their sexual intimacy?

UNDERSTANDING THE TEXT

6. How do the initial verses of this section of the Song of Songs indicate that the lovers are progressing toward the consummation of their

marriage (4:8–11)? What evocative phrases, words, and images does the man use, in these four verses, to evoke the delight of sexual intimacy?

7. What would you say the pictures of a "locked garden" and an "enclosed fountain" tell us about the young man's bride (4:12 TOTC)? How does this verse call back to and reaffirm the warnings that we have heard thus far in the Song of Songs?

8. What images and pictures does the man use as he continues to celebrate his intimacy with the woman he loves—and what senses do they involve (4:13–15)? How do these verses further develop the picture of marital delight and consummation in this passage?

No Double Standard, pg. 86

There is no double standard: both men and women alike are to restrain their sexual desire until and within marriage. This is not because God is harsh and restrictive, or has imposed laws designed to prevent human flourishing. Quite the contrary: such restraint is the precise means whereby the delightful fruitfulness, unique intimacy, and glorious rest that a sexual relationship was designed to bring can be fulfilled.

9. In 4:16, the woman responds to her husband's desire. In what way does her response differ from her previous words of warning and caution—and what is the reason for this change?

10. Note the man's response to his wife's joyful invitation (5:1). How do the "daughters of Jerusalem" then celebrate and affirm their love? What can this teach us about the role God's people play in the marriages of others?

11. This passage portrays a rightly ordered enjoyment of sexual pleasure in the place that God has ordained for it, and thus it should not make us uncomfortable. What does sexual pleasure teach us about our God? What does it teach us about the eternal delights and pleasures that God's people will experience in the presence of their Savior?

BIBLE CONNECTIONS

12. Read Genesis 2:25, which describes the marriage relationship that Adam and Eve shared before the fall. How does this passage from the

Song of Songs beautifully demonstrate the same lack of shame within marriage and sexual intimacy? What does this tell us is still possible for marriages that take place after the fall?

13. In Psalm 16, David affirms that there are "pleasures forevermore" at God's right hand (v. 11). What do such verses tell us about life in the new heaven and new earth?

THEOLOGY CONNECTIONS

14. Our God chose to make sex pleasurable and enjoyable. He also intends for it to be enjoyed only within the commitment of marriage. What does this teach us about the character and heart of God?

15. Answer 72 of the Westminster Shorter Catechism, in its explanation of the seventh commandment, cautions against all "unchaste thoughts, words, and actions." How does the passage that we are studying model chaste speech even while celebrating sexual intimacy within marriage?

APPLYING THE TEXT

16. What does the fact that this passage is *in the Bible* indicate about God's view of sexual intimacy and enjoyment when it is in the context of marriage? In what way, if any, do your own views in this area need to change in order to better align with God's?

17. Even as this passage offers us a positive view of sex, what implicit warning should we take from it about sexual sin? Why must Christians be firmly committed to pursuing sexual purity and restraint?

18. The mutual love, satisfaction, and delight that are found in a good earthly marriage pale in comparison to the love that Christ has for his people. Why is this encouraging news for people, whether married or unmarried, who have faced frustration or disappointment in their pursuit of intimacy?

Love for Sexual Strugglers, pg. 95
It will be a lifelong struggle to pursue obedience in our sexuality, one in which we will often fail. In those times, we need to come back again to the cross, to remind ourselves of God's unshakable, burning love for us. We are all repeat offenders who are in desperate need of his grace. But as we behold God's incomparable love for us—the legal, affectionate, and passionate bond that, in Christ, he has entered into with his creatures—we find the love that we so crave.

PRAYER PROMPT

As you close your study of this passage, ask God to make you more joyfully committed to his plan for sexual purity. If you are married, ask God to help you to be satisfied joyfully and contentedly with your spouse. If you are not married, ask him to allow you to find joy and contentment in sexual purity for his glory. No matter your marital status, pray that God would remind you of the passionate love he has for you—a love that will never grow cold or fade away, because it has been made possible through Christ.

LESSON 9

INTIMACY LOST AND REGAINED

Song of Songs 5:2–6:3

THE BIG PICTURE

After the glorious wedding celebration, and the intimate and delightful consummation of the marriage that followed, we come to a passage with a noticeably different tone. It is probably best understood as a dreamlike portrayal of the types of barriers to love and intimacy that a married couple face. Married life is not perfect! As the desires of the husband and wife run hot and cold, the sins and frustrations that can threaten a human relationship are on full display.

At the beginning of this dreamlike sequence, the husband seeks intimacy with his sleeping wife, but she prevents him—perhaps by locking him out of the bedroom (5:2)! The woman continues to hold him at a distance as she questions why she should go to him (5:3–4). Her mindset changes, though, and her desire for intimacy with her husband returns—but by then he has gone away (5:5–8).

The ensuing description of her nighttime search for him through the town (and the abuse she suffers along the way) is most likely a continuation of this dream—as well as a poetic picture of the pain and frustration that can be involved in the pursuit of ongoing intimacy. During her pursuit, the woman responds to the questioning daughters of Jerusalem in a way that evidences her renewed appreciation and desire for her husband and that especially celebrates his physical appearance (5:9–16). As the daughters of Jerusalem ask, "Where has your beloved gone?" the woman finally discovers him, and the passage ends as she offers a renewed expression of the mutual belonging that is theirs through the bond of marriage (6:1–3).

This passage shows us the real frustration, pain, and struggle that can complicate a marriage after the wedding festivities have ended and real life begins. There is more here, though. We see again a picture of the emotional and spiritual distance that our selfish and sinful desires can put between our Savior and us. Marital love is to be guarded, protected, and pursued; it is worth fighting for! And we are to pursue our relationship with Christ with the same fervency—for he is the great Bridegroom who has pursued us and will never let us go.

Read Song of Songs 5:2–6:3.

GETTING STARTED

1. An overly idealized view of marriage will set the stage for major disappointment. What steps should an engaged couple take to help them to set realistic expectations for what life will be like after their wedding?

2. What obstacles, in your heart and in your life, make it difficult for you to enjoy deeper intimacy with God?

No Perfect People, pg. 98

There are no perfect people to marry—only deeply flawed sinners who will sometimes disappoint you, hurt you, and let you down. What is more, we, too, are deeply flawed sinners who will fail and disappoint our spouses in a thousand different ways. That is what this portion of the Song of Songs is about: the glorious intimacy that the lovers entered through marriage is threatened and lost for a time, before finally being restored after a lengthy search.

OBSERVING THE TEXT

3. What clues within the text suggest that this passage is depicting a dream?

4. The woman's tone changes and shifts continually throughout this passage. What turning points can you identify within it, and what emotions do they reveal?

5. What role do the daughters of Jerusalem (who are referred to here as the "Others," in the ESV) play in this passage, and what are their interactions with the woman like?

UNDERSTANDING THE TEXT

6. With what words does Song of Songs 5:2 establish this section's dreamlike quality? What does it portray the husband desiring?

7. What kind of tone do you detect in the wife's response to her husband (5:3)? What reasons does she give for turning down his advances? What does he do in response—and what effect do his actions have on his wife (5:4)?

8. What vivid events and details accompany the woman's frantic pursuit of her husband, after her desire for him has returned (5:5–8)? What do you think these images are teaching us about the danger and pain that can be involved when we pursue intimacy?

9. After holding him off emotionally and physically, the woman again desires her husband (5:9–16). What does she celebrate about him? What familiar emotions have returned to her speech?

10. Note the realization that finally puts an end to the woman's frustration and frantic pursuit (6:2). How is this stress-inducing dream resolved?

11. What important idea does the woman return to as the passage concludes (6:3)? Her statement illustrates the beauty of the mutual belonging and self-giving that take place between spouses in a Christian marriage. What does this tell us about our relationship with God?

BIBLE CONNECTIONS

12. Read Paul's teaching in 1 Corinthians 7:4. What does he tell the Corinthians about married men and women? What makes this selfless attitude important to a healthy marriage relationship?

13. Read James 4:8, which contains a beautiful promise about God's response to humble sinners who "draw near" to him. What hope does this verse bring to those who have been distant from God?

We Are All Relentlessly Self-Absorbed, pg. 105
This poem challenges us to see all the ways that we behave in our relationships as though "my beloved is mine and I am mine as well." We constantly act as though we belong to ourselves and rule over our own little kingdoms, which others may enter, but only if they wish to bow down and serve us. . . . If we are honest, we are all relentlessly self-absorbed.

THEOLOGY CONNECTIONS

14. The Westminster Confession of Faith describes the duty Christians have to "marry only in the Lord" (24.3). Why is it important for followers of Jesus to seek only believing spouses? Considering the difficulty that is inherent to any marriage, why is it so crucial for both spouses to be devoted to Jesus, as long as one of them is?

15. During our study of the Song of Songs, we have been frequently reminded that Jesus Christ is our ultimate "Bridegroom" and that the people of God are betrothed to him. This is not meant to be a strange or sexual picture; it is rather a reminder that our ultimate desires for intimacy, love, delight, and joy will be satisfied by our Savior, forever and ever. How can a healthy marriage serve to remind us of this glorious reality? And how can a marriage that is full of *struggle*, as well as the pain of loneliness, also remind us of this spiritual truth and hope?

A Lifelong Pursuit, pgs. 98–99

Entering marriage is not the end of your search for a spouse. It is the beginning of a lifelong pursuit, as you continually sin against each other, and then ask for forgiveness, pushing through the obstacles that threaten to divide you in search of true intimacy. The same is also true, of course, of your relationship with God through Christ, to which human marriage provides a God-given analogy.

APPLYING THE TEXT

16. What does this passage tell us about marriage relationships? What can this teach you about your need for God's grace when you are in a relationship with another fallen human being?

17. How can this text help to encourage you as you pursue your walk with your great Bridegroom, Jesus Christ? What struggles, sins, and challenges get in the way of intimacy between you and your Savior? What can you do to confront them in order to prayerfully continue to seek God and walk with him?

18. In what way can this passage be a helpful corrective to idealized views of romance and marriage—and a reminder of the divine love and relationship that God's people experience?

PRAYER PROMPT

As you end your study of this passage, ask God to help you to be patient in and committed to your relationships with fellow redeemed sinners. If you are married, pray to be able to show grace, patience, and the kind of sacrificial love for your spouse that exalts Christ. If you are not married, pray that God would continue to give you strength and help, through his Spirit, so that you can continue to love and obey your Savior, whatever obstacles you face.

LESSON 10

MAKING UP IS HARD TO DO

Song of Songs 6:1–12

THE BIG PICTURE

This next section of the Song of Songs, beginning in verse 4, is challenging to translate. As we seek to understand it, we'll revisit the setup provided within the previous lesson, from 6:1–3, for some helpful context. The man and the woman, after their agonizing waiting and longing, have been married and enjoyed both the celebration and the consummation of their covenantal union. They have endured their first marital conflict and now know the pain of interrupted intimacy and hurtful words and actions. Now, as our next passage opens, the woman wonders if the sweetness of their relationship can be restored. Can this couple lovingly and graciously make up?

In response, the man immediately—and completely—reassures the woman with loving words of comfort (6:4–10). He tells her, in essence, that he still loves her, still thinks she is beautiful, and still is as smitten by her as ever. Her beauty is awe-inspiring and even overwhelming to him (vv. 4–5). The man again uses metaphors from nature to describe his beloved's features and form (vv. 5–7). He concludes by affirming his wife's uniqueness and incomparability (vv. 8–10). The man's speech takes its full effect as it comforts his doubting wife and reassures her of his love, his commitment, and his desire for her.

While there is some disagreement about the right way to interpret the woman's words in 6:12, it does seem that what she discovers in the "garden" where she meets the man (6:11 TOTC) leads them to experience enthusiastic and reassuring delight in their love once again. The conflict in their relationship has actually made it stronger. In a similar way, we often find that times of testing and struggle in our spiritual lives drive us to love, trust, and worship our beloved Savior all the more.

Read Song of Songs 6:1–12.

GETTING STARTED

1. Think of a time when you saw the devastating effects of unresolved conflict on a friendship or marriage. What holds people back from extending forgiveness—or asking for forgiveness?

2. How has God used struggle, pain, conflict, or restlessness in your life to drive you to have a deeper faith and trust in him? How has he shown his deep love for you—even during these times of doubt and trial?

Grace, pgs. 120–21

Have you ever been in the woman's situation here? You have sinned against someone you love intensely and know that you deserve to receive coldness, anger, and harshness from him or her. Yet instead, what you actually received was love, acceptance, and warm forgiveness. What an amazing and joyful experience that is!

OBSERVING THE TEXT

3. Look again at 6:1–3 for context. In what ways do the woman's heart and behavior seem to change in response to the simple questions asked by the "daughters of Jerusalem"?

4. In what ways are the words the man speaks to the woman in 6:4–10 similar to what we have seen before in the Song of Songs? What is different about them? How does he communicate the intense passion he has for his wife—and the incomparability he sees in her?

5. In 6:11–12, how do the husband and wife seem to resolve and conclude their relational conflict? Where in these verses do we see the celebration of a restored relationship?

UNDERSTANDING THE TEXT

6. How does the woman's response to the question from the "daughters of Jerusalem" indicate that she hopes to restore her relationship with her beloved (6:1–3)?

7. What does the man affirm about the woman in 6:4–5? How does he describe the effect that she has on him?

8. What pictures from the natural world does the man employ as he heaps reassuring praises on his wife (6:5–7)? What makes these similar to pictures we have seen before in this book? What is new about them?

9. What different metaphors and images does he employ in 6:8–10 to celebrate the regal beauty of his beloved? How does the man show that his wife is absolutely unique to him—that she is set apart from every other woman in the world?

10. What important aspect of the relationship between Christ and the church is demonstrated by the man and the woman in this passage?

11. What seems to surprise the woman as she goes down to the "garden" (6:11–12 TOTC)? What emotions does verse 12 suggest that she is experiencing?

BIBLE CONNECTIONS

12. In Colossians 3:13, the apostle Paul offers a simple command to God's people: "As the Lord has forgiven you, so you also must forgive." Where in this lesson's passage do you see the husband obeying this command? What does his attitude tell us about Christ's?

13. In what ways do you see this passage poetically illustrating, and arguing for, the way spouses should work through marital problems and remain committed to each other? How does Jesus's teaching in Matthew 19:9 reinforce this argument?

Healing Words, pg. 115

What caused this transformation from the cautious but fearful optimism with which the woman entered the garden, hoping to find some buds of their love left intact, to such expressions of rapturous delight? It was the words that the man said to her, which are recorded in verses 4–10. In other words, the man's response to their conflict blew her away.

THEOLOGY CONNECTIONS

14. Answer 33 of the Westminster Shorter Catechism explains that, through "justification," our God "pardons all our sins, and accepts us as righteous in his sight." How can the way the man lovingly celebrates his wife in this lesson's passage serve as a picture for us of the way our gracious God not only "pardons" us but even "accepts us as righteous" in his sight?

15. The traditional teaching of the church (based on Matthew 19) has been that Christians may get divorced only in cases of adultery or desertion (which is sometimes interpreted to include abuse as well). The church emphasizes the importance of preserving a marriage commitment—even during difficult times. How does this lesson's passage support this teaching?

God Welcomes Our Return, pg. 125

When we come to our senses and recognize our own sin, turning back to God from our repeated pursuit of our idols, perhaps we are still fearful of what we may find. We are unsure whether there will be a welcome for us after the ways in which we have sinned and let him down. Yet what we discover from our God when we return to him is nothing less than his unique and unchanging love and affirmation.

APPLYING THE TEXT

16. What can this passage teach us about the power and beauty of forgiveness—when it is practiced not only in marriage but in any loving friendship or relationship?

17. Why must we make the gospel of Jesus Christ the motivation for our forgiveness, restoration of relationships, and conflict resolution? How can the grace God has shown us as sinners motivate and guide us to forgive others when we are wronged?

18. If you are married, what gospel truths are important for you to remember whenever you and your spouse deal with conflict? Regardless of your marital status, what has this passage taught you about confessing sin, practicing forgiveness, and working toward restoration when a relationship is strained?

PRAYER PROMPT

Human relationships are messy. We hurt, wound, and offend one another in our marriages and our friendships—and often we don't even do it on purpose! Today, pray for God to give you the grace to seek and extend forgiveness and to work toward restoration in your relationships, whenever possible. Ask him to remind you of the abounding grace he has shown you, a sinner, through the work of his Son. Thank him for the fact that, even when you become distant from him, he welcomes you back when you confess and humbly return to him!

LESSON 11

AND SO (ONCE MORE) TO BED

Song of Songs 6:13–8:4

THE BIG PICTURE

Our last lesson left off as the husband and wife reconciled after a marital conflict—the couple has made up, and love and harmony have been restored to their relationship. Depending on the translation being consulted, this next passage picks up either with the husband calling to his wife to come to him or with the chorus summoning her (6:13). An extended speech follows in which he celebrates his wife's physical beauty and describes his overwhelming admiration for her (7:1–9). His beloved is, in a word, *perfection* in his eyes. Images from both the natural world and human craftsmanship dominate his speech—from gazelles, trees, and luscious fruit to fancy ornaments, bowls of wine, and mighty towers—forming a picture of abundant and lively love. The man adores his wife and proclaims her beauty . . . as well as his sexual desire for her, which becomes explicit toward the end of the speech (vv. 8–9).

The woman responds with enthusiasm (7:9–10) and suggests that the two of them go together to find a beautiful spot in nature where they can enjoy love and intimacy (7:11–13). She concludes by reiterating her longing for intimacy and her desire for the privacy of her family's dwelling, since the couple must not display their love and affection in public (8:1–3). Finally, once again, out of this loving ecstasy and intimate delight emerges a warning—the woman cautions against awakening this kind of powerful love before its right time and outside its right place (8:4).

We find in this passage a man and woman unashamedly celebrating sexual love, and enjoying each other's bodies, in the good and right context of marriage. Sexual intimacy and pleasure fill this passage in God's Word—and God does not seem to be ashamed by this! Yet we should lift our eyes past the fleeting earthly delights described in this passage to the eternal delight that lies ahead: the pleasures that Psalm 16 says are at the right hand of our God. God's people look ahead to the physical, embodied, resurrection life they will forever enjoy in the presence of their great Savior and Bridegroom!

Read Song of Songs 6:13–8:4.

GETTING STARTED

1. How does our culture—and especially the entertainment industry—inappropriately put sexual pleasure on full display? How have you seen Christians respond when this is done?

2. Why is it important for followers of Jesus to maintain a proper view—and theology—of the body? What is lost when we emphasize the spiritual and forget that God has a plan for his physical creation—including for our bodies?

God Is Not Embarrassed, pg. 130

God is concerned about . . . what we do with our bodies. So God is willing to do what some commentators are not: to talk to us about our bodies and our sexuality. God is not embarrassed by such subjects, and neither should we be embarrassed by them. Equally, though, the Word of God is not crass and crude when it talks about sex. It treats the body with an appropriate poetic modesty and restraint that we should try to respect.

OBSERVING THE TEXT

3. Did anything surprise you about this text as you read through it? Does it shock you that this passage is contained in the Holy Scriptures? Why, or why not?

4. What makes it clear that this section of the Song of Songs is focused on sexual enjoyment and satisfaction? And yet what does it do to cover its sexual descriptions with a layer of modesty—and even restraint?

5. In this section, the husband and wife display mutual commitment, satisfaction, and joy. What words and phrases give evidence of this?

UNDERSTANDING THE TEXT

6. In his translation of the Song of Songs, Iain Duguid attributes all of 6:13 to the husband. When we look at the verse in that way, what do we see the man doing to further convince his wife that he fully forgives, accepts, and desires her (6:13)?

7. What does the man primarily celebrate in 7:1–7 about the woman he loves? What images and metaphors does he use to do so? What can these verses teach us about the kinds of ways that married couples can praise and compliment each other?

8. The man clearly expresses his intentions and desire for his wife in verse 8 through the beginning of verse 9. What makes it clear that his desire is explicitly sexual?

9. The woman responds to the man's desire for her in the rest of verse 9 through verse 13—how would you describe her response? In what ways does she also express her own desire? What does she suggest that they do?

10. As the woman continues her speech, she expresses her desire for intimacy with the man she loves (8:1). What longings does she articulate in 8:2–3?

11. What warning does she direct to the daughters of Jerusalem (8:4)? How has the context of this warning changed since the last time she issued it to them?

BIBLE CONNECTIONS

12. Read Hosea 2:1–13, and note the imagery it uses to depict Israel. What connection do these prophetic words make between our human marriages and our divine "marriage" to our God? According to Hosea 2, how does sin impact our standing before God?

13. The bridal imagery in Revelation 21:1–3 is very different from the imagery in Hosea 2! Read through those verses. What transformation have the people of God undergone? What has made this transformation possible? What does it illustrate about the gospel?

Sex Is a Mutual Blessing, pg. 137

Sex was invented by God to be delightful in its own right as a way to bless your spouse and for him or her to bless you. It wasn't intended to be fun for men and a necessary nuisance for women; on the contrary, it was supposed from the beginning to be a mutually enriching experience of great joy for both.

THEOLOGY CONNECTIONS

14. Answer 108 of the Heidelberg Catechism calls every Christian to "detest [unchastity] from the heart and live a chaste and continent [meaning self-restrained] life both within and outside of holy wedlock." What protection do a husband and wife have against unchastity? What positive alternative to sexual sin have you seen in this passage we have been studying?

15. The man's words in Song of Songs 7:1–7 focus almost exclusively on the body and *physical* beauty of his wife. While the physical beauty we see on earth will fade, and while our bodies (and marriages) are temporary and mortal, God's people do have hope that the physical creation will be renewed—and that our bodies will be resurrected to everlasting physical life. How should this knowledge serve to temper any obsession we have with physical beauty? What attitude should we have toward God's physical creation and our own (and others') bodies?

We Need a Better Husband, pg. 139

What this means is that sex, even great sex within a wonderful marriage, is not enough. A stunningly beautiful body is not enough. We need a better Husband, who gives us a perfect beauty, in which he then delights—an eternal Husband who loves us with an intensity of passion of which human sexuality is only a pale reflection.

APPLYING THE TEXT

16. How should we apply the warning we encounter at the conclusion of this passage (8:4)? Why do you think the woman is again urging caution regarding sexual intimacy, even within her marriage? What can we learn from this?

17. If the sexual delight and desire that this passage describes are truly part of God's design, then what does this teach us about our God? How can what we learn about him shape our anticipation of what is to come when we experience physical, resurrected life in the new heavens and new earth?

18. How does the passion that the husband shows for his wife illustrate Christ's passionate love for his church? In what ways does Jesus demonstrate this love? How can the way the woman responds to her husband in this passage serve as a model for the way we should respond to Christ?

PRAYER PROMPT

Human beings, and human sexuality, are created by a good God who delights in the eternal pleasure of his people. Today, pray for God to ground your understanding of human sexuality and intimacy more deeply in an understanding of what the end and final trajectory of all earthly joy and delight will be: eternal pleasure in and with Jesus Christ, the King and Savior. If the topic of sexual intimacy brings you frustration, pain, or longing, take joy in the fact that your eternal fulfillment will be in Christ. If you enjoy healthy sexual intimacy in the context of marriage, pray for God to use that, too, to draw you to worship him, obey him, and long for his eternal presence all the more.

LESSON 12

LOVE AND DEATH

Song of Songs 8:5–7

THE BIG PICTURE

In the brief passage we will study in this lesson, we see the woman looking beyond the physical enjoyment of sexual intimacy and toward deeper reflections on the power—and pain—of human love. Several different images arise within this passage, as the woman reflects on her love for her husband and continues to ponder the passion and strength of their bond.

As the woman is pictured coming up from the "wilderness," she is leaning on her husband—presenting a picture of companionship, support, and mutual belonging (8:5). The next brief image this passage evokes—a love scene, which takes place underneath an "apple tree"—portrays the woman's memory of her first experience of sexual intimacy with her husband during their marriage (v. 5). She quickly connects sex to childbearing, though, as she looks back on the generation that came before them, whose own love gave life to children. The woman's earnest desire for commitment, and even her jealous loyalty, give way to the passage's next image: a "seal" upon her husband's heart (8:6). As she continues to reflect on their passionate and loving commitment to each other, she evokes one final image: a blazing flame of fire. Their love burns both hot and steadily with passion, loyalty, jealousy, and commitment! As she concludes her speech, the woman speaks for everyone who deeply loves another person: those who know such love would not trade it for any amount of wealth the world has to offer (8:7).

This passage focuses on themes we have already seen, yet it also widens and deepens them. In these verses, the woman ponders the power, passion, and strength of her love for her husband—and of his for her. The passage brings to life for us the wonder and depth of such human love and leads us again to ponder the depths of the love our gracious God has for sinners such as us. His love is unbreakable, unquenchable, rich, and full—and we see it most beautifully at the cross of his Son.

Read Song of Songs 8:5–7.

GETTING STARTED

1. When have you witnessed love leading to pain, hurt, heartbreak, or even violence? What does this tell you about love's power and its influence in our lives?

2. What warnings have godly and wise people in your life given you about love, romance, or sex? What made those warnings helpful?

The Glory and Pain of Love, pg. 145
Throughout the Song, we have seen the most glorious descriptions of love side by side with stern warnings against stirring up love too soon. In this passage, as we reach the poetic climax of the Song, the glory and pain of love are once again starkly portrayed side by side in a series of distinct but related images.

OBSERVING THE TEXT

3. What themes and pictures appear in this text that are familiar from elsewhere in the Song of Songs?

4. Who is the only speaker in this text? What different images does the speaker use—and what different themes do these images seem to suggest?

5. What vivid details does the woman use to describe the striking power of love? What does she seem to desire from her husband?

UNDERSTANDING THE TEXT

6. This passage begins with the woman coming up from the "wilderness" (8:5). What might this image be symbolizing? What parts of the biblical narrative does it echo?

7. In the next line, the woman leans against her husband and is supported by him. What aspects of marriage does this image evoke?

8. What is the language in the middle of verse 5 clearly describing? Why is it right for the woman to celebrate this moment?

9. What can we learn from the connection the woman makes between the two things she mentions in 8:5? What dangers do we face when we try to divorce these things from each other?

10. How does the woman communicate the power and passion of love at the end of verse 6 and the beginning of verse 7? What makes these images helpful? What do they teach us about the power of love—and also about the danger and pain it can involve?

11. The woman's speech closes with a statement, near the end of 8:7, about the incomparable wealth and value of love. Have you ever experienced

the truth of this statement? Why must we feel this way all the more deeply about the love we have for *God*—and what does the statement tell us about his own powerful and deep love for us in Christ?

BIBLE CONNECTIONS

12. Read 1 Peter 3:1–7, and note the love, respect, and even gospel witness that Peter calls wives and husbands to live out within marriage. What kind of beauty does Peter encourage godly women to display?

13. Once again, the fierce and fiery love we see between this man and this woman reminds us of God's love for us—and our love for him. Read Psalm 42:1–2. How does the psalmist model what a passionate love for God, as well as an earnest pursuit of fellowship with him, look like?

Love Is a Commitment, pg. 146

Love is not just a sweet union of two souls journeying peacefully from the wilderness into the promised land of family life. It is a lifelong and unique commitment, an insatiable appetite that cannot be tamed, placated, bought, or sold. We have seen some of these challenges on our journey through the Song of Songs. Love demands to possess its beloved and to be possessed by him in a unique way.

THEOLOGY CONNECTIONS

14. The woman uses the language of a "seal" (8:6) to describe the strong and binding covenant commitment she and her husband have made with each other. Why is it important for Christians to understand the role of a "covenant" in a marriage? How do the covenantal promises and commitment that marriage entails enable us to more clearly see the covenant love God has shown us in Christ?

15. If our chief purpose as humans is not only to "glorify God" but to "enjoy him forever," what might the seemingly unquenchable nature of romantic love be designed to teach us about our future with God (WSC 1)? Why is it important for us to remember that our call is to both give glory to God and also *enjoy* him?

Friendship on Fire, pg. 151

In Jesus, we truly experience friendship on fire. For Jesus to win his spouse, it was not enough for him merely to humble himself and come to earth to be our friend. . . . Jesus had to do far more than that in order to win us as his friends forever. . . . Jesus didn't just live the life of perfect love to give us an example to follow; he lived it *for us*, in our place.

APPLYING THE TEXT

16. We have seen that sexual pleasure needs to be deeply connected to commitment, loyalty, and even childbearing. How can Christians emphasize these connections for the good of those around them?

17. Because love is intensely powerful, we must handle it carefully. What does this passage encourage and challenge you to do in your particular life situation?

18. The fiery descriptions of love that this passage contains point us past human love to *divine* love. Why is it important for us to remember that God's love is ultimate—and is the only love that will eternally satisfy us?

PRAYER PROMPT

We have seen in this lesson that human love is powerful. Today, thank God for the deep, loving relationships in your life. Your friendships, family relationships, and marriage (if applicable) are good gifts from a loving God! Let this passage inspire you to praise and adore the God who loves you with unquenchable love, which he demonstrated most fully at the cross of his Son—who laid down his life for you. Ask him to help you to be passionately, deeply, joyfully committed to loving, worshiping, and serving Jesus—your Savior.

LESSON 13

THE SONG THAT NEVER ENDS

Song of Songs 8:8–14

THE BIG PICTURE

In this final passage of the Song of Songs, we are confronted with several different scenes that each illustrate aspects of romantic love, marriage, and the community that surrounds a marriage. These scenes are not to be understood in chronological sequence; they are rather giving the reader some final illustrations of community, covenantal commitment, and God's good gift of marital love as the book concludes.

The chorus speaks up first. Whether they are referred to as "brothers" (TOTC) or as "others" (ESV), they comment on the protective role that they filled in their younger sister's life prior to her marriage day and celebrate the sexual purity and patience she showed until God's appointed time arrived for sexual intimacy (8:8–9). The woman picks up on the chorus's illustration of a "wall" and describes the commitment she made to chastity until the day of her marriage (8:10). We next move on to a song about "vineyards"—both King Solomon's rich and expansive vineyard and the vineyard that belongs to the humble young woman (8:11–12). The young woman celebrates the simple love and commitment that she finds in her home and marriage, which are more valuable to her than the immense, lavish riches of a king such as Solomon. Finally, we are brought back to a dialogue between our two main characters (8:13–14). The man calls to the woman in the "gardens"—the place of love (v. 13). The woman tells him to "make haste" and somewhat mysteriously references "mountains of spices" (v. 14). Most likely, she is affirming the love to which they are committed—even when they are apart—while also celebrating their desire for intimacy with each other.

The Song of Songs ends, then, with familiar themes: sexual purity, the incomparable riches of true love, and desire and commitment within a marriage—all of which are affirmed by a loving community. The book leads us to consider, again, the way that God designed human love and marriage to point us to his love for us—his bride—which has been demonstrated through the covenant goodness and mercy of his Son.

Read Song of Songs 8:8–14.

GETTING STARTED

1. What are some benefits you have seen from the influence of older Christian siblings on younger ones? How have you seen this dynamic play out, in a church context, between older and younger "siblings" in Christ?

2. Anyone who has truly and deeply loved another person knows that money and wealth cannot compare to that experience. What does this tell us about the love of God?

The Nature of the Life of Love, pg. 156
[The Song of Songs] does not close with a neat and tidy conclusion but rather with a return to the beginning, picking up some of the central themes from along the journey and rounding off in a way that leaves us hungry for more. . . . It is a deliberate strategy to push us to think about the nature of the life of love that the poet has described throughout this book, in terms of both our human relationships and our relationship with God.

OBSERVING THE TEXT

3. What main breaks divide this final passage in the Song of Songs? What alerts you to the fact that these verses are describing several different scenes?

4. Who are the main speakers in this passage, and what are their functions? What specific role does the chorus seem to be playing?

5. What seems to be the tone of the interactions that the man and the woman have with each other, one final time, here at the close of the book? What are their desires and hopes, and how do they express their love for each other?

UNDERSTANDING THE TEXT

6. What does the imagery that the chorus uses to describe the young woman indicate about her behavior and attitude before she was married (8:8–9)? What do you think these verses suggest about the role that

people's families and Christian communities play in both promoting sexual purity and urging holiness and sexual restraint?

7. As the woman picks up on the chorus's imagery (8:10), what is her tone? Why must we understand that a commitment to protecting purity is a good thing—not a restrictive or joyless endeavor?

8. What seems to be the point behind the woman's description of the vineyard of Solomon (8:11)? What connection do you see between her focus on the tremendous wealth of this vineyard and earlier scenes we have studied in the Song of Songs?

A Precious Gift, pg. 162

[Sex] is a precious gift of God that exists in service of a unique, lifelong, committed bond between one man and one woman in which she both brings and finds peace in his eyes. Sex is designed to bond a couple together in marriage so that she completes him and he completes her. As the book of Genesis puts it, "Therefore a man shall leave his father and his mother and hold fast to his wife, and they shall become one flesh" (Gen. 2:24).

9. As the woman contrasts her own vineyard with Solomon's, how do her words in 8:12 show that she is contented and satisfied with what belongs to her? What message does she seem to be communicating about the value and wealth of simple love?

10. The man lifts his voice one last time to call out to his beloved as the Song draws to a close (8:13). How does he express his desire for her—and what familiar imagery does he evoke in his call to her?

11. The final verse of the book seems to portray the woman's acknowledgment of the distance that will sometimes come between her and the man she loves ("make haste, my beloved") along with her desire for ongoing intimacy with him ("mountains of spices"). What does this final verse teach us about the role that the covenant commitment of marriage plays in varying seasons of life?

BIBLE CONNECTIONS

12. Both the young woman and the chorus use the picture of a "wall" to evoke an image of sexual purity, restraint, and guardedness. What vision does Titus 2:11–14 give us for battling "worldly passions"? Who helps us in this fight, and how?

13. Read 1 Timothy 5:1–2. How does Paul encourage the young pastor to whom he is writing to treat younger women in the church—and what connection do you see between this advice and the behavior of the chorus in Song of Songs 8:8–9?

THEOLOGY CONNECTIONS

14. This passage reminds us of the call God has given us to guard sex and enjoy it only within the context of marriage. What does the "wall" imagery illustrate, on a spiritual level, regarding our relationship with God?

15. Answer 66 of the Westminster Larger Catechism explains that our union with Christ is "the work of God's grace, whereby [we] are spiritually and mystically, yet really and inseparably, joined to Christ as [our] head and husband." What does this tell us about our deepest identity? How should our union with Christ lead us to think about human marriage?

APPLYING THE TEXT

16. What does this passage teach us about the role that Christian family members ought to play in our lives and romantic relationships? How can older siblings, or mature older believers in the church, help to train and encourage younger generations in matters of sexual purity?

Come to the True Lover of Your Soul, pg. 167

So how will you respond to God's amazing love? Perhaps . . . you are still married to your idols, even though they treat you like a slave and constantly leave you deeply unsatisfied. Leave them, and come to the true Lover of your souls. Give your heart and life over to him, and find in him a true peace that transcends the difficulty of your present circumstances.

17. What can you learn from the woman's contentment with her own "vineyard" and her satisfaction in her home and loving marriage? If God is calling you to be more content with some relationships in your life—whether they are earthly or spiritual—then in which of your relationships does your contentment need to grow?

18. How does this final passage of the Song of Songs point us to the deep love of Christ? In the course of this study, what have you learned about the role Christ's love ought to play in your life and relationships?

PRAYER PROMPT

As you close your study of the Song of Songs, spend some time in prayer. Ask God, the ultimate Lover of your soul, to give you the strength and help, by his Spirit, that you need in order satisfy yourself in him. Ask him to remind you of his burning love for you, which you can see most clearly through the cross of his Son, Jesus Christ. Pray to be able to love the people around you—your spouse, your family, your friendships, and the community of God's family—with a strong and joyful love that is shaped by God's love for you.

Jon Nielson is senior pastor of Spring Valley Presbyterian Church in Roselle, Illinois, and the author of *Bible Study: A Student's Guide,* among other books. He has served in pastoral positions at Holy Trinity Church, Chicago, and College Church, Wheaton, Illinois, and as director of training for the Charles Simeon Trust.

Iain M. Duguid (PhD, University of Cambridge) is professor of Old Testament at Westminster Theological Seminary in Philadelphia. He has written numerous works of biblical exposition, including *Daniel* in the Reformed Expository Commentary series, *Ezekiel* in the NIV Application Commentary series, and *Numbers* in the Preaching the Word series.

Did you enjoy this Bible study? Consider writing a review online.
The authors appreciate your feedback!

Or write to P&R at editorial@prpbooks.com with your comments.
We'd love to hear from you.

P&R PUBLISHING'S COMPANION COMMENTARY

Should we read Song of Songs as romantic poetry—or as an allegory? Should some people even read it at all? Pastor-scholar Iain Duguid steers a middle way between allegorical and literal approaches and shows that this book's celebration of the love between a man and woman not only shapes Christians' thinking about human relationships but also reveals the love that Christ has for his bride, the church.

The Reformed Expository Commentary (REC) series is accessible to both pastors and lay readers. Each volume in the series provides exposition that gives careful attention to the biblical text, is doctrinally Reformed, focuses on Christ through the lens of redemptive history, and applies the Bible to our contemporary setting.

Praise for the Reformed Expository Commentary Series

"Well-researched and well-reasoned, practical and pastoral, shrewd, solid, and searching." —**J. I. Packer**

"A rare combination of biblical insight, theological substance, and pastoral application." —**Al Mohler**

"Here, rigorous expository methodology, nuanced biblical theology, and pastoral passion combine." —**R. Kent Hughes**